Everyday Witness

A Journey of Sharing Faith

LEADER'S GUIDE

STEPHEN HANCE

Church House Publishing
Church House
Great Smith Street
London SW1P 3AZ

www.chpublishing.co.uk

Published 2022 by Church House Publishing

Copyright © The Archbishops' Council of the Church of England 2022

ISBN 978 1 78140 297 9

The opinions expressed in this book are those of the author and do not necessarily reflect the official policy of the General Synod or The Archbishops' Council of the Church of England.

A catalogue record for this book is available from the British Library

Concept and design by www.penguinboy.net

Printed in the UK by

Contents

"The highest and most beautiful things in life are not to be heard about, nor read about, nor seen but, if one will, are to be lived."

SØREN KIERKEGAARD

....

This is for you – if you could do with some encouragement in living your faith.

This is for you – if you know Scripture is full of stories which relate to your life but aren't quite sure where to start.

This is for you – if you recognise that you are a witness but wonder why God didn't think of a more effective way.

We are all called and sent as witnesses of Jesus.

Everyday Witness takes this as truth, and then sets us on our way in living it. It is a wonderful resource and I urge you to pick it up and engage with it.

This will help all of us live our faith.

ARCHBISHOP JUSTIN WELBY

Welcome to Everyday Witness

In Acts chapter 1, just before the ascension of Jesus, we read that he said this to his disciples: 'You will receive power when the Holy Spirit has come upon you; and **you will be my witnesses** in Jerusalem, in all Judea and Samaria, and to the ends of the earth' (Acts 1.8, emphasis added).

This isn't just a message for the people who heard Jesus on that day. It's a message for all those who think of themselves as followers of Jesus. But to lots of us, it sounds a bit mysterious or difficult – or even scary. What is a witness anyway? How would I become one . . . or am I one already? Does it mean I have to become one of those super-confident people who never seem to be shy about sharing their beliefs with others?

Of course, the disciples who heard this message had been on a journey of learning and growing with Jesus. This was the final commission, not the first one. And they had been on a journey together, sharing their hopes and dreams, and their setbacks and mistakes.

So we, too, are going to embark on a journey together to learn how we can be witnesses. The structure of **Everyday Witness** is inspired by the National Health Service's 'Couch to 5k' fitness model, which has become very popular. The genius of 'Couch to 5K' is that it recognizes the only way for non-runners to become runners is to **run!** No amount of inspiring books or motivational videos will make someone a runner. It is beginning to run, beginning with just the tiniest distance, that makes someone a runner. 'Couch to 5K' is practicable and active from the very beginning.

This approach is one we have borrowed for **Everyday Witness**. From the beginning, we won't just think about being witnesses to Christ. We will begin to put into action what we have learned. We will do it gently; we will do it together; and we will do it with the Holy Spirit as our helper.

How to Use Everyday Witness

Everyday Witness works at three levels:

1. for the whole church
2. for the small group
3. for the individual.

Each level will work on its own to some extent. So if you don't know anyone else who is doing **Everyday Witness**, you could use the individual materials on your own. Or perhaps you're in a small group that would like to do it, although your whole church isn't currently doing it. In this case, you could use small-group and individual materials, and so on. Two key points, though: the individual materials, and the actions that come out of them, are crucial parts of the programme, so you probably wouldn't get much out of it without using those. And, whenever possible, it is best to take this journey together, with a home group, the whole church or just a few friends. The different resources are described here.

Sunday-service resources

Every week has some prompts to use when planning the weekly service.

This is not a script but a series of suggestions. Feel free to use all or some, as you wish. Sunday-service resources include passages from the Bible that you could use instead of, or as well as, the lectionary readings; possible hymns and songs in a range of styles and traditions; suggested additional liturgical elements, such as a testimony or interview; and a few thoughts that can feed into the sermon.

You will find that **Common Worship** has other resources which tie in with these themes: for example, special collects and intercessions for mission and evangelism in **Common Worship: Festivals**, pages 342 and following.

Home-group resources

As with the Sunday-service resources, these are best approached as a menu from which you can pick and choose rather than a recipe that must be followed precisely. You will want to bear in mind whether a group is new, formed for this season only or well established with strong relationships already. Some small groups may meet for two hours or more, to have social time together; others will want to keep the gathering to sixty minutes. Some home groups may now be online.

There will be different levels of confidence with prayer, sharing or reading aloud, which a good leader will be attentive to. Most of the home-group materials consist of suggestions to discuss certain things. When there is a section simply to be read out to the whole group, it is clearly marked.

A typical structure for an hour-long home group meeting might be as follows:

- Scripture reading (10 minutes)
- input (5 minutes)
- discussion (15 minutes)
- activity (20 minutes)
- prayer and end (10 minutes)

There is a collect – a 'gathering' prayer – for use at the end of each home-group session. It is the same each week, and we hope that people might get to know it well and pray it regularly.

Daily reflections

The material for the individual is found in the accompanying **Everyday Witness: Reflection Journal** from Church House Publishing.

Each week there are five days' worth of reflections. You might use them every morning, Monday to Friday, perhaps on your way to work or over a cup of coffee. You can read these or hear them being read. Each day will include a short section from the Bible, a reflection, perhaps a brief story, a prayer and a suggested activity for the day. The stories are drawn from real life, but names and identifying details have been changed. The activities are important. They can make the difference between a course that simply gives us new information or an experience that builds our confidence as witnesses and followers of Jesus.

If you are doing **Everyday Witness** with a home group, or you have a friend doing it as well as you, you could set up a WhatsApp group or agree to text each other each day to talk about how you have got on with these actions.

Everyday Witness is a journey and, like every journey, it begins with a single step.

So let's begin!

Week 1
The Story
of God

Sunday Service Resources

The theme for this week is the story of God. Behind all the stories we know from the Bible, there is one big story: the story of God and God's engagement with the world. This week, we explore this story and begin to think about our place in it.

Exploring the theme of the service

MOST PEOPLE WHO ATTEND CHURCH REGULARLY probably know a good number of Bible stories, and even people who don't may remember some of the best-known ones from school. But behind all those individual stories, there is a big story that runs like a thread through the Bible. It's the story of a good and loving God who creates a beautiful world, and of creatures made in God's image who then go their own way and corrupt themselves and God's creation. God calls a people to know him in a special way, with the aim of blessing the whole world. In time, he liberates those people from slavery, leading them to a land of their own. Sadly, the pattern established at the very beginning, of turning away from God, continues. The people insist on a king because they want to be like other nations and, when it all goes wrong, they end up in captivity again. This time there is no dramatic moment of rescue, but a promise that a Saviour will come to make things right. When Jesus appears on the scene, some people recognize him as God's Saviour, even though he doesn't seem to fit a lot of common expectations about that special person. Jesus is crucified and most conclude that this is the end of the story. Instead, it turns out to be just the beginning. Jesus is raised to life again and returns to heaven, sending and equipping his followers to represent him in the world. Those who believe in him continue to trust that, one day, Jesus will return and all will be made right.

Sociologists call a big story such as this a 'metanarrative'. We don't need to know that word, but we do need to understand something of the shape of this big story so that we can understand how our own stories connect with it, and so that we can invite other people to connect their stories with it, too. While this is a very broad sweep to cover in one service, it will be important to help people to get a sense of the big story of God as we begin the **Everyday Witness** journey.

Over the next few weeks, we will be encouraging the telling of stories. Perhaps you might begin this week by asking someone to share (briefly!) something of the story of your church.

- How did your church begin?
- What have been a few of the key moments?
- How have you seen God at work? And what does that tell you about God's purpose for you?

Prayers

Eucharistic Prayer D from **Common Worship** would be appropriate today.

Music

Suitable hymns and songs could include:

- I will sing the wondrous story
- Come, thou long expected Jesus
- Our God reigns
- O for a thousand tongues to sing
- This I believe
- We believe (Graham Kendrick)

Readings

You may find the lectionary readings are all that you need to focus on these themes. Here are some suggested alternative texts that you could use alongside the lectionary readings:

- Genesis 12.1-3
- Psalm 137.1-6
- Acts 9.18-22
- Revelation 21.1-4

Home-Group Resources

Read Genesis 1.1-5, 26-31; 3.1-19

If you have time to read the whole of Genesis 1 and 3, even better.

Introducing the theme (to read aloud)

MOST PEOPLE WHO ATTEND CHURCH REGULARLY probably know a good number of Bible stories, and even people who don't may remember some of the best-known ones from school. But behind all those individual stories, there is a big story that runs like a thread through the Bible. It's the story of a good and loving God who creates a beautiful world, and of creatures made in God's image who then go their own way and corrupt themselves and God's creation. God calls a people to know him in a special way, with the aim of blessing the whole world. In time, he liberates those people from slavery, leading them to a land of their own. Sadly, the pattern established at the very beginning, of turning away from God, continues. The people insist on a king because they want to be like other nations and, when it all goes wrong, they end up in captivity again. This time there is no dramatic moment of rescue, but a promise that a Saviour will come to make things right.

When Jesus appears on the scene, some people recognize him as God's Saviour, even though he doesn't seem to fit a lot of common expectations about that special person. Jesus is crucified and most conclude that this is the end of the story. Instead, it turns out to be just the beginning. Jesus is raised to life again and returns to heaven, sending and equipping his followers to represent him in the world. Those who believe in him continue to trust that, one day, Jesus will return and all will be made right.

The first chapters of Genesis give us the first part of the story. They contain good news and bad news, and identify the problem that the rest of the Christian story seeks to address. God creates, with tenderness, love and unbridled imagination, and a universe comes together that is full of wonder and possibility. The pinnacle of this this cosmos-making is the creation of humanity, designed to reflect the image of the creator in a unique way and charged with joining God in the co-creation of gardens, cities and culture.

Unfortunately, it doesn't work out that way. One of the earliest acts of the human race is to decide that we have a better way of doing things than God's way, and the consequences are severe. Sickness, sin and isolation enter into the created order, and our relationships with God and with one another are torn.

Thankfully, this is not the end, but it sets us up for all that is going to happen as the story unfolds.

Discussion

What strikes you as you read and reflect on these early verses of Genesis? Does this picture of a wonderful creation gone wrong resonate with your experience of the world around you? If so, how important would it be for something to happen to make things right?

Activity

During this week, we have been invited to think about the people around us and to choose five whom we can pray for regularly, trusting that they might come to faith in Christ. If you feel comfortable, share with others in the group about whom you are praying for. Without disclosing anything sensitive or confidential, tell the others a little bit about them and where you think they might be in terms of openness to faith. What opportunities do you think there might be to talk to them about your own faith?

It might be sensible to agree a time limit, say three minutes each, and appoint someone to signal when there are only thirty seconds left. Or you might do this in smaller groups of three or four.

When everyone who wishes to speak has done so, talk about how you feel concerning the prospect of sharing your faith with your five others. What would stop you or make it difficult for you? Can you think of some ways of beginning that conversation?

Prayer

Spend some time in prayer together, thanking God for your 'fives' and the ways God is already at work in their lives. And pray for one another, that God would give you opportunities to speak about him and courage when those opportunities come along. You can pray out loud or in silence, as you prefer.

Collect

Lord Jesus, you send us out
into your world to be your witnesses
in the things we say and do.
Grant us the help of the Holy Spirit
that we may point people to your love,
and so bring glory to you.
Amen.

Looking ahead

Over this week, we will look at some key moments in the big story that the Bible tells. This is the story of God's involvement with the world – with us. This is our story.

Reflections for Individuals

The ***Everyday Witness: Reflection Journal*** offers daily readings, reflections, prayers and actions to help us travel further in our individual journey of sharing faith.

In this first week it explores the theme of 'The Story of God' through the following readings:

Monday	Exodus 3.7-12
Tuesday	1 Samuel 8.1-7
Wednesday	Psalm 137.1-6
Thursday	Isaiah 42.1-4
Friday	Matthew 3.13-17

Week 2
The Story
of Us

Sunday Service Resources

The theme for this week is the story of us. We are not merely individuals on our own, as our culture seems to suggest. Instead, we are 'in Christ', part of something much bigger than ourselves, and members of the Body of Christ, deeply connected with one another. The call to witness is a call to **us**, not just to **me**.

Exploring the theme of the service

THE TEACHING OF THE CHURCH is that, through faith, baptism and reception of the Holy Spirit, we are all 'in Christ'. Because we are in Christ, our personal story becomes part of the Church's story and indeed of God's story.

This entails a fundamental change of identity. We live in a culture in which identity is central. Our culture's concept of identity tends to be individualistic and self-chosen. The Bible shares, with most cultures in world history, a concept of identity that is much more communal. Identity is about belonging. Learning to live within our new identity is a lifelong journey. In this service, you may want to consider how you could invite people to step into that new identity for themselves or to renew their commitment to it.

Readings

You may find the lectionary readings are all that you need to focus on these themes. Here are some suggested alternative texts that you could use alongside the lectionary readings:

- Psalm 107.1-32 (or a shorter section, such as verses 1-9)
- Acts 2.37-47
- Galatians 3.23-29
- John 3.16-22

Other

It would be good to add a regular 'story' or 'testimony' slot to the service over these few weeks. This week, perhaps you could begin by asking one person (in advance) to share how he or she first came to your church.

Music

Suitable hymns and songs could include:

- All my hope on God is founded
- Be thou my vision
- The Church's one foundation
- Be still, for the presence of the Lord
- Before the throne of God above
- O Jesus, I have promised

Prayers

In the liturgy, you may wish to include the renewal of baptismal vows, perhaps accompanied with the sprinkling of water as a reminder of baptism. The Proper Preface and Blessing from the Baptism service in **Common Worship** are appropriate for use in this service.

Home-Group Resources

Read Matthew 1.1-17

Introducing the theme (to read aloud)

I HAVE HEARD A VERY GREAT NUMBER OF SERMONS in my life, most of which I can't remember. But one I remember very clearly, even though I heard it more than twenty years ago. I was visiting a central London church for the evening service, which turned out to be a service of adult baptism. When the time came for the Bible reading, someone stood and read the genealogies from the beginning of Matthew's Gospel. At verse 17, the reader stopped and sat down, and I wondered what on earth the preacher was going to make of this passage. The preacher talked us through some of the names in the list, highlighting some of the lesser-known characters or those who made terrible mistakes, as well as some of the heroes of the faith. After several minutes, he turned to those who were to be baptized and said, 'Today, your name gets added to this list. Today, your story becomes part of this story of those who have passed through this world in relationship to God. Today, you connect your story with God's story.'

Last week, we thought about the story of God and God's activity in the world, through creation, the Fall; the calling of Abraham; the Exodus; the giving of the Law and the sending of the prophets; the life, death, resurrection and ascension of Jesus; the outpouring of the Holy Spirit and the birth of the Church: all moving forwards towards the return of Christ as King and the renewal of heaven and earth. This week, we are thinking about our own stories of faith and how, through faith in Christ and baptism into his people, our stories become part of God's story, too.

Activity

During this week, we have been invited to think through and write down something of our own life stories, highlighting key moments. In your group, take a little time now to share some headlines from your stories with one another. You will have to be selective, otherwise it could take a long time! You shouldn't feel under any pressure to share things that you don't want to share or, indeed, to share at all. It might be sensible to agree a time limit, say three minutes each, and appoint someone to warn when there are only thirty seconds left.

When everyone who wishes has done this, talk about what you have heard.

Have you noticed how significant moments in another person's story have helped to make that person who they are today? Where does God fit in to these stories? This is not the same as asking, 'When did this person become aware of God?' or 'When did these individuals start to talk about God as they told their stories?' It may be that you can see how God was involved even though religious language wasn't used at all. Did you get a sense of the times when this person's story and God's story connected in a particular way? Was there a clear moment of coming to faith in Christ or did that happen in a more gradual way?

Prayer

Spend some time in prayer together, thanking God for what you have learned about one another and for the ways in which your stories are connected to his story. Pray that you might become more aware of that connection in the future. You can pray out loud or in silence, as you prefer.

Collect

Lord Jesus, you send us out into your world to be your witnesses in the things we say and do. Grant us the help of the Holy Spirit that we may point people to your love, and so bring glory to you. Amen.

To Read Aloud

When we talk about witnessing to our faith, sometimes we get quite anxious because we think that means being able to explain the gospel like a theologian or being able to answer hard questions about our faith. But that's not what being a witness means. Witnesses tell the story of their own experience, what they have seen and heard, no more and no less. We live in a culture in which beliefs and truth claims are debated and contested, but in which stories are welcomed and listened to.

Reflections for Individuals

The **Everyday Witness: Reflection Journal** this week explores the theme of 'The Story of Us' through the following readings:

Monday	Psalm 107.1-32
Tuesday	Romans 6.1-11
Wednesday	Romans 8.1-11
Thursday	1 Corinthians 12.12-27
Friday	Matthew 5.13-16

Looking ahead

Today, we have been reminded that we each have a story and that God is part of that story. This week, write down briefly the story of how your faith came alive and what difference that has made to you, in such a way that you could share it with somebody else. Make sure that it can fit on one sheet of paper, and that you can read it out in two or three minutes. You may need to do this more than once to be happy with it. Bring your piece of paper with you to next week's meeting.

Week 3
God's Witnessing Love For All

Sunday Service Resources

The theme for this week is how God's love and offer of salvation are for everyone. From the very beginning, God's intention has been to bring all people into restored relationship with him. The vocation of the people of God in the Old Testament and New Testament alike is to reveal God to the whole world. Jesus supremely takes that vocation upon himself and fulfils it.

Exploring the theme of the service

AS THE PEOPLE OF THE EARLY CHURCH reflected on the life, death and resurrection of Jesus, they came to understand quite quickly that all this meant God's saving love was offered to the whole world. The gift of the Holy Spirit to Gentiles in Acts 10 made this very clear. This would have been a distinctive viewpoint in the religious landscape of the time. But it also meant that there was something distinctive for Christians to do, in bearing witness to the God they had encountered in Jesus. They bore witness in the way they lived together, in the radical hospitality they offered and in their speaking about Jesus and what he had done. As God's people today, we are called to do the same.

It would be good to continue with a regular 'story' or 'testimony' slot in the service over these few weeks. Perhaps you could ask someone who has lived overseas to share how his or her faith developed there.

Readings

You may find the lectionary readings are all that you need to focus on these themes. Here are some suggested alternative texts that you could use alongside the lectionary readings:

- Genesis 22.15-18
- Psalm 103.1-5, 19-22
- Acts 11.1-17
- John 1.1-13

Music

Suitable hymns and songs could include:

- In Christ there is no East or West
- He's got the whole world in his hands
- From the rising of the sun
- Our God reigns
- Ye servants of God
- In Christ alone
- To God be the glory

Prayers

In the liturgy, you may wish to add some elements from the Church in other parts of the world. If your congregation includes people who come from outside the UK or if you have links to other countries through, for example, mission societies you support, you might like to use some prayers from a prayer book from one of those regions.

Do bear in mind that the Church of England Canons require the use of authorized forms for certain elements of the liturgy, especially at Holy Communion (such as the words of absolution, profession of faith, Eucharistic Prayer and blessing). There is generally more scope at A Service of the Word for using material drawn from outside **Common Worship** or **The Book of Common Prayer**.

Home-Group Resources

Read Acts 10.1-48

Introducing the theme *(to read aloud)*

STEPHEN HANCE, the main author of **Everyday Witness**, tells this story.

> *Several years ago, I was at a Christian conference in a very non-touristy town on the west coast of the USA. One evening, after the conference session was over, a friend and I dropped into a nearby bar for some pizza and beer. The place was busy, so we sat up at the counter and ordered. Our English accents gave us away, of course, and we found ourselves being quizzed by other people who were propping up the bar: mainly younger, alternative types, with tattoos and piercings. They wondered what were we doing in a place like this. So we told them. We were in town for the Christian conference at the convention centre. Our new friends were stunned. Christians? Drinking beer and chatting with them in their run-down bar? Surely Christians didn't want to hang around in places like that, with people like them? As the conversation went on, it turned out that, for them, Christians were on a long list of people whom they didn't like, whom they wouldn't associate with and whom they would even judge and condemn. I left feeling sad that Christians had given these people such an impression.*

Last week, we thought about some of the key moments in our own stories. We also explored how, through faith in Christ and baptism into his people, our stories become part of God's story, too, and we will return to this later in the session. This week, our subject is about God's witnessing love for all.

Discussion

What strikes you as you listen to these verses from Acts? Take some time to share your thoughts. And remember, there are no 'right' or 'wrong' answers.

To read aloud

At different times and in different ways, religious people can begin to think of themselves as the 'in crowd': those who have been chosen by God for special status in his kingdom and who can therefore look down on others, the 'outsiders'. Those US friends had no doubt experienced some of this from certain Christians. Our Bible readings this week remind us how misplaced this view is. God's love is for everyone; his purpose is for everyone; and his family is open to everyone. Even when God does call a particular group of people – Israel in the Old Testament and the Church in the New – that calling is for the sake of others, so that God's goodness and glory might be reflected in the world. So we are Christians not only for ourselves but also for others, to bear witness to God's love and longing for everyone.

Activity #1

During this week, we have been invited to think about the people around us: those we find it harder to imagine becoming Christians, as well as those we can easily imagine coming to faith. We have been invited to engage in faith conversations with some of these people. If you feel comfortable doing so, take some time now in your group to share how that has gone for you this week.

What have you done? What has happened? What have you learned?

It might be sensible to agree a time limit, say three minutes each, and appoint someone to warn when there are only thirty seconds left.

When everyone who wishes to has done this, talk about what you have heard.

- Are there encouraging stories here?
- How do they help you to think about being a witness in your own life?
- Where can you celebrate that God has been at work?
- What has surprised you about that?
- Have some people in the group found this particularly challenging or had negative experiences?

Activity #2

If you have time, you can do this activity, too. If you wish, you can do it instead of Activity 1.

Last week, we discovered that we each have a story and that God is part of that story. During the week, you were asked to write down briefly the story of how your faith came alive and what difference that has made to you, in such a way that you could share it with somebody else. Now, give an opportunity, for those who would like to, to read what they have written.

Prayer

Spend some time in prayer together, thanking God for the people you have spoken to this week and the ways God is at work in their lives. Pray for anybody with whom a group member has had a particularly good conversation. Pray for new opportunities to bear witness to God's love for all in the week ahead. Pray that you might become more aware of that connection in the future. You can pray out loud or in silence, as you prefer.

Collect

Lord Jesus, you send us out into your world to be your witnesses in the things we say and do. Grant us the help of the Holy Spirit that we may point people to your love, and so bring glory to you.
Amen.

Looking ahead

The God who loves us loves everyone and wants each person to come to know him. The stories we tell are part of the way that God is revealed to others. Over the coming week, ask people you know to share something of their stories of faith with you. It doesn't matter whether they are Christians or something else. Why do they believe what they do? Why does it matter to them? If they ask, be prepared to respond by telling your faith story.

Reflections for Individuals

Readings used in the **Everyday Witness: Reflection Journal** this week:

Monday	Isaiah 49.5-6
Tuesday	Acts 8.26-38
Wednesday	Acts 11.17-18
Thursday	Acts 13.46-49
Friday	John 3.16-17

Week 4

Discovering the God Who Goes Before Us

Sunday Service Resources

The theme for this week is discovering the God who goes before us. Rowan Williams is quoted as saying that 'mission is about seeing what God is doing and joining in'.[1] This week, we are thinking about what it means for God to take the initiative in mission: that the Spirit is always ahead of us, working in ways visible and invisible, inviting us to share in that life-giving work.

Exploring the theme of the service

IN THE PARABLE OF THE banquet, a wealthy man has planned a wonderful party and invited all the great and the good of the area. But in the event, all the important, invited guests have other things to do. So the host flings wide the doors and sends out a messenger to invite literally everybody, whoever they might be.

We get a picture of God who is not content to include just the powerful, wealthy or even religious people, but who throws open the doors of the heavenly party and sends out to invite everyone in, whoever they may be and wherever they may come from.

But don't forget the vital role of the messenger. Without his going into the streets and giving the message that the banquet is here and the doors are open wide, nobody would have known to come. St Paul makes the point that if we have truly understood the love of Christ for us, then we will feel compelled to share that love with others, in word and deed.

Pope Francis, in **Evangelii Gaudium (The Joy of the Gospel)**, writes:

> The primary reason for evangelizing is the love of Jesus which we have received, the experience of salvation which urges us to ever greater love of him . . . If we do not feel an intense desire to share this love, we need to pray insistently that he will once more touch our hearts . . . What then happens is that 'we speak of what we have seen and heard' (1 John 1:3). The best incentive for sharing the Gospel comes from contemplating it with love, lingering over its pages and reading it with the heart.[2]

Evangelism, at its simplest, is opening ourselves to the love of Christ to such an extent that this love cannot help but overflow and touch those around us.

We have previously encouraged you to add a regular 'story' or 'testimony' slot to the service over these past few weeks. Perhaps, today, there might be someone able to share how they have come across signs of God at work in surprising or hidden ways in your community.

Readings

You may find the lectionary readings are all that you need to focus on these themes. Here are some suggested alternative texts that you could use alongside the lectionary readings:

- Genesis 12.1-3
- 2 Corinthians 5.11-15
- Luke 14.16-24

Music

Suitable hymns and songs could include:
- **Amazing grace**
- **From all the wind's wide quarters**
- **Banquet (There's no banquet so rich)**
- **There's a wideness in God's mercy**

Prayers

We have used a weekly collect in the home-group resources. You might like to use it in your service this week.

Lord Jesus, you send us out into your world to be your witnesses in the things we say and do. Grant us the help of the Holy Spirit that we may point people to your love, and so bring glory to you. Amen.

Home-Group Resources

Ice-breaker

Try to think of a time when you came across a situation where it wasn't clear what was going on or where, perhaps, you initially misunderstood what was happening. Perhaps there was a crowd gathering, people shouting or someone running. What did you think was happening at first? What did the real story turn out to be? Hopefully, at least one or two people in the group will have an example to share with the others. Give the group a few minutes to think and then to share whatever has come to mind. If there are several of you, you might want to do this in smaller groups of about three.

Discussion

The former Archbishop of Canterbury Rowan Williams is quoted as saying that 'mission is about seeing what God is doing and joining in'.[3]

Take a few moments to discuss what you think the quote means. How does it make you feel? Do you agree with it? How do we find out what God is doing?

Introducing the theme (to read aloud)

ARCHBISHOP ROWAN'S quote reminds us that whenever we think about mission, evangelism or witnessing about our faith, God is already ahead of us. God is a missionary God, always reaching out in love to the whole creation.

Mike Starkey, Head of Church Growth in Manchester Diocese, tells a story about hidden leopards.

> Here's a true story from South Africa. Some game wardens from a safari park were transporting a leopard. The van got into an accident and the leopard bounded off into the suburbs of Johannesburg.

> So, the game wardens called in hunters to trap the leopard before it caused any damage.
>
> The hunters arrived with their rifles and searched the suburbs for a wild leopard. And on their very first night of searching, they found **seven** leopards all hiding in the suburbs. In other words, at least six leopards had been there all along. It's just that nobody had been looking for them!
>
> To me, that story says something about God at work in my community. What if God's already out there, touching hearts and lives? In other words, what if God's like those leopards in the suburbs of Johannesburg? There all the time – it's just that we haven't noticed.[4]

If this is true, it means that God is already out ahead of us, working in our communities and in the lives of individuals.

So have a think together about this. What 'hidden leopards' – unobtrusive signs of God at work – are you aware of now? They could include a conversation that very naturally led to talk of God, new people joining in with church online or an open door for some kind of outreach in the community. Talk about what comes to mind.

Scripture

The Message version of Luke 10.1–9 is suggested and reproduced here:

Later the Master selected seventy and sent them ahead of him in pairs to every town and place where he intended to go. He gave them this charge:

'What a huge harvest! And how few the harvest hands. So on your knees; ask the God of the Harvest to send harvest hands.

'On your way! But be careful – this is hazardous work. You're like lambs in a wolf pack.

'Travel light. Comb and toothbrush and no extra luggage.

'Don't loiter and make small talk with everyone you meet along the way.

'When you enter a home, greet the family, "Peace." If your greeting is received, then it's a good place to stay. But if it's not received, take it back and get out. Don't impose yourself.

'Stay at one home, taking your meals there, for a worker deserves three square meals. Don't move from house to house, looking for the best cook in town.

'When you enter a town and are received, eat what they set before you, heal anyone who is sick, and tell them, "God's kingdom is right on your doorstep!"'

Discussion *(to read aloud)*

Jesus seems to be telling us that when we go on his mission to share his good news, sometimes we will come across people who will welcome us and our message. He considers them people of peace. These peace-people are those in whose lives God is already at work, making them ready to find out more about him and to recognize his work in them. They may not call themselves Christians or go to church, but they are prepared for the next step on their journey towards God. This isn't by luck or chance but because God the Holy Spirit has been working, quietly and unobtrusively – like a 'hidden leopard'!

In your discussion, talk about how you respond to this idea. Can you think of 'people of peace' you have encountered? What difference does it make to how you think about being a witness when you remember that God is already going ahead of you?

Collect

Lord Jesus, you send us out into your world to be your witnesses in the things we say and do. Grant us the help of the Holy Spirit that we may point people to your love, and so bring glory to you.
Amen.

Prayer

Pray for those 'people of peace' you can think of and others whom you haven't spotted yet. Ask God to give each of you the chance to speak with a person of peace this week. Pray for the ability to spot the 'hidden leopards', signs of God at work all around you. And perhaps allow a few minutes of silence in prayer to be attentive to the whisper of the Spirit and share anything that comes to mind afterwards.

Looking ahead

This coming week, pay close attention to those unobtrusive signs of God at work around you.

Reflections for Individuals

Readings used in the **Everyday Witness: Reflection Journal** this week:

Monday	Luke 4.16-21
Tuesday	Luke 7.36-50
Wednesday	Romans 8.19-23
Thursday	John 12.31-33
Friday	1 Corinthians 15.21-24

Week 5
Our Calling
to the World

Sunday Service Resources

So far, we've thought about God's story and our own stories, and the way God is at work in the world. This week, we think about our calling as witnesses about Jesus Christ in the places where we spend most of our time each week, from Monday to Saturday (what many call their 'frontline'). This may be the community, the family, or your work at home or elsewhere. Many of us have multiple 'frontlines' and God is calling us to witness about him on all of them. But what might our witness on our 'frontlines' look like? How might we bear fruit for God, day by day, wherever we are?

Exploring the theme of the service

ONE EXCELLENT WAY OF MAKING SURE OUR WORSHIP reminds us of our calling to the world is to use an idea from the London Institute for Contemporary Christianity (LICC) – the introduction of a regular slot in the Sunday service called 'This Time Tomorrow'. Each Sunday, one member of the congregation talks about what he or she will be doing this time tomorrow (that is, on Monday morning). The individual shares the challenges and opportunities faced at work, in the family or in the community (wherever his or her 'frontline' is – the place where the person spends the most time when not in church). Someone then prays for the church member, leading the congregation in prayer.

To launch 'This Time Tomorrow', you could invite a number of people from the congregation, with different callings and 'frontlines', to bring an object to the service that represents a dimension of their calling to the world, and ask them to talk about it for a couple of minutes. This could be repeated over a period of time to begin to build up a picture of the range of situations in which the congregation spend their daily lives.

Readings

You may find the lectionary readings are all that you need to focus on these themes. Here are some suggested alternative texts that you could use alongside the lectionary readings:

- Jeremiah 29.1-7
- Psalm 24
- Acts 1.1-11
- Matthew 5.13-16

Prayers

We introduced a collect last week which you might like to continue to use.

*Lord Jesus, you send us out
into your world to be your witnesses
in the things we say and do.
Grant us the help of the Holy Spirit
that we may point people to your love,
and so bring glory to you.
Amen.*

Music

Suitable hymns and songs could include

- O Jesus, I have promised
- Brother, sister, let me serve you
- Everyone needs compassion
- All I once held dear

Home-Group Resources

Introducing the theme *(to read aloud)*

WE ALL HAVE A 'FRONTLINE' . . . even if we don't think we do. After a sermon one Sunday, a lady in her eighties told the vicar that she didn't think she had a 'frontline'. A couple of minutes of chat later and she realized that she did. She was a member of the local Women's Institute and she knew that they all watched her to see what difference being a Christian made! There was her opportunity to bear witness; a gift and calling from the Lord.

Ice-breaker

What are your 'frontlines'? Talk with one other person in your group and see if you can help each other to see where God is calling you to be a witness for him.

Scripture

Read John 15.1-11

This is part of Jesus' so-called 'farewell discourse' to his disciples. There is a sense that he is communicating vital instructions to them as he prepares them for life without his physical presence. So these instructions are particularly important as a guide for us as his followers.

Discussion

The image of the vine is one with a history in the Old Testament. Take a look at Isaiah 5.1-7, in which Israel is pictured as God's vineyard. How does Isaiah 5.7 help us to understand what being fruitful looks like? Think, too, about the seed-bearing purpose of fruit in nature. Jesus tells the disciples that they will only bear fruit if they abide in the vine – in him. What does it mean to be 'apart' from Jesus (John 15.7) and conversely to 'abide' (or 'remain') in him? While thinking about your 'frontlines', can you identify times when you have borne fruit for God? What has that fruit looked like?

Here are some pointers:

- Jesus suggests that abiding in him primarily involves obedience to his commandments and instructions. So we bear fruit when we are obedient.

- Mark Greene suggests six key areas in which we can bear fruit on our 'frontlines' (each of which reflects Jesus' instructions in the Gospels):

  1. **modelling** godly character;

  2. **making** good work;

  3. **ministering** grace and love;

  4. **moulding** culture;

  5. being a **mouthpiece** for truth and justice;

  6. being a **messenger** of the gospel.[5]

- Which of these (you can choose more than one) seems especially relevant to you on your 'frontline'?

Activity

Spend some time discussing which of the six areas of obedience to Jesus are particularly relevant on your 'frontlines'. For instance, you might see a glaring need for justice for fellow employees. Alternatively, you might know of a situation in which doing one of these things made a real difference that others saw and appreciated. Where are the challenges for you on your 'frontline' this coming week?

Prayer

Spend some time praying for one another as you seek to abide in Jesus from Monday to Saturday. This could be done altogether or in smaller groups of two or three; out loud or in silence.

Collect

Lord Jesus, you send us out into your world to be your witnesses in the things we say and do. Grant us the help of the Holy Spirit that we may point people to your love, and so bring glory to you. Amen.

Looking ahead

Notice what difference it makes to how you feel, speak and act when you think of your Monday-to-Saturday life as your 'frontline'.

Reflections for Individuals

Readings used in the **Everyday Witness: Reflection Journal** this week:

Monday	Genesis 2.15-17
Tuesday	Ephesians 1.3-14
Wednesday	Genesis 41.1-45
Thursday	Daniel 3.8-18
Friday	Acts 8.26-40

Week 6
Witnesses and Evangelists

Sunday Service Resources

The theme for this week is the understanding that, because of our baptism, we are all Jesus' witnesses. Drawing on Jesus' words in Acts 1.8 and his promise that we **will** be his witnesses, the important questions to ask are, 'What **kind** of witness am I?' and 'What **kind** of witnesses are we?'

Exploring the theme of the service

VERY OFTEN, WE COUNT OURSELVES OUT of sharing our faith because we have in mind a caricature of what an evangelist looks like. The distinction between witnesses and evangelists in the New Testament helps us to let go of the unhelpful picture of an evangelist that we may have. It also encourages us that we can all bear witness to what God has done in our lives. Similarly to Peter and John in Acts 4, our hope is to become people who cannot help but speak about the things we've seen and heard.

Alongside the focus on personal witness, this service could help the congregation reflect on their communal witness. How does life together as a community bear witness to the God revealed in Christ?

Readings

You may find the lectionary readings allow you to focus on these themes. Here are some suggested alternative texts that you could use alongside the lectionary readings:

- Psalm 66.16-20
- Acts 1.1-8
- Acts 4.1-22
- Ephesians 4.1-13

While the main focus of the service will be on our shared call to witness, there will be some who have been called to the office of evangelist. You may want to help to identify what that might look like in a person's life and draw out the idea from Ephesians 4 that an evangelist is one who equips people for works of service. You could encourage those who feel called to this particular ministry to begin a process of exploration.

Music

Suitable hymns and songs could include:

- Take my life and let it be
- Amazing grace
- At the name of Jesus
- To God be the glory
- Oceans (Where feet may fail)
- Follow you
- King of my heart
- Send me out

Prayers

Perhaps this week you could include some prayer for evangelists. If you are aware of people with this gift in your congregation, there could be a liturgical act of blessing or commissioning.

Home-Group Resources

Read Acts 4.13-20

Introducing the theme (to read aloud)

Rich, one of the authors of this session, says:

> Whenever it comes to choosing which film to watch in our house, if the option is there for a courtroom drama, that will get my vote. Maybe it's because I grew up with thoughts about working for justice in society by being a lawyer. Perhaps it was because I was simply gripped the first time I watched Alec Baldwin shout 'You can't handle the truth!' in **A Few Good Men**. In movies, law courts are depicted as places of drama and intrigue. This fiction was shattered when I had to do my civic duty and enrol for jury service. After two weeks of waiting around, I finally became part of a jury for a very dull case. The difference between the movies I love and what I saw while on jury service was the distinction between the role of the lawyer and the witness.

When we think about the idea of being **evangelists**, many of us are put off. It may be because we've seen one too many televangelists and street-corner preachers or simply because we don't think we know enough to share our faith. In the lawyer–witness analogy, we picture an evangelist as a bit like a lawyer. We think we need to know all the details of the case, the fine elements of the argument and be quick on our feet in case we're caught out. However, the majority of us are not called to be evangelists but witnesses. We see an example of this in the passage in Acts. In this reading, we note that

1. Peter and John were recognized as 'uneducated and ordinary' people who had spent time with Jesus;

2. Peter and John simply spoke about what they had 'seen and heard'.

In other words, Peter and John did what all witnesses do in a courtroom. They testified to what they had seen and heard. They were living with the promise in mind that Jesus had made to them at the start of Acts, when he said you **will** be my witnesses.

Activity

Discuss together or in smaller groups the following two questions.

1. How does the analogy of lawyer and witness help you to understand the difference between the evangelist and the witness?

2. As you reflect on your whole life, what kind of witness do you think you currently are? What kind of witness would you like to become?

To read aloud

There is a famous quote, often attributed to Theodore Roosevelt: '**Comparison** is the **thief of joy**' (emphasis added). It can be far too easy to get lost in comparing ourselves to everyone else. In the process, we either end up becoming arrogant, as we think we're better than others, or falling into low self-esteem because we think we're worse than everyone else. It's no different when we think about witnesses and evangelists. Not all of us are called to be evangelists; yet we are all called to witness. As Paul writes in 1 Corinthians 12.20: 'There are many members, yet one body.' How each of us goes about the task of being a witness will look different, depending on the situations we find ourselves in. The important point is to recognize that we are **all** witnesses for Jesus, individually and corporately.

How can we spur one another on in our roles as witnesses for Jesus? In what ways can we encourage one another to speak about the things we've seen and heard? And for those of us who have been gifted as evangelists, how can we use that gift of the Holy Spirit to help to equip us all in our witness concerning the good news of Jesus Christ?

Prayer

Spend some time praying together. Thank God for how he has made us all differently and wants to work through each person's personality and character as we witness to others about Jesus. Pray that we might grow in our willingness to be witnesses. Pray also for those gifted as evangelists to have a greater sense of that call on their lives. You can pray out loud or in silence, as you prefer.

Collect

*Lord Jesus, you send us out into
your world to be your witnesses
in the things we say and do.
Grant us the help of the Holy Spirit
that we may point people to your love,
and so bring glory to you.
Amen.*

Looking ahead

Be attentive to the opportunities that come along this week to witness about your faith in words or action. How do you feel at those moments? When do you think that you have made the best use of them?

Reflections for Individuals

Readings used in the **Everyday Witness: Reflection Journal** this week:

Monday	John 4.28-42
Tuesday	John 9.13-34
Wednesday	Ephesians 4.11-13
Thursday	1 Corinthians 12.12-31
Friday	Luke 17.11-19

Week 7

Engaging with the Place of Witness

Sunday Service Resources

The theme for this week is encouraging people to engage with the world around them. Drawing on concepts explored in Week 1, Week 4 and Week 5, the aim is to help us all to live as disciples of Jesus who are not 'of the world' and yet have been sent as witnesses **into** the world.

Exploring the theme of the service

THE IDEA OF STORY HAS RUN throughout **Everyday Witness**. This week, we explore the idea of the interaction between the big story of Scripture and the stories of the culture we inhabit. There have been different Christian responses to the prevailing culture throughout history. They are generally found somewhere on a spectrum between full cultural assimilation and becoming a community completely closed off from the surrounding culture.

Drawing on the idea that, in the beginning, God created everything and saw that it was good, we aim to see that the world around us, while damaged, is still God's good creation awaiting its redemption. It's a place we can expect to find the Lord at work. At the same time, the big story of Scripture reminds us that all humanity has been made in the image of God. While that image may be marred, part of our witness is pointing to where we see the image of God in the people around us or something of the truth, goodness and beauty of God in the surrounding culture.

The aim of the service will be to encourage us all to become 'detectives of the divine', growing in attentiveness to the ways in which God's Spirit is at work in the people and culture we inhabit, and learning to witness about that work.

Readings

You may find the lectionary readings are all that you need to focus on these themes. Here are some suggested alternative texts that you could use alongside the lectionary readings:

- Ezra 1
- Psalm 104 (or some of it)
- Acts 17.16-34
- Romans 8.18-30
- Matthew 8.5-13

This week, perhaps you could ask someone to share a story of a time when he or she has discovered God's Spirit at work in an unexpected place or through an unexpected person. This could have been through a piece of art or music; it may have been through creation or in the actions or words of someone who wasn't a Christian.

Music

Suitable hymns and songs could include:

- There's a wideness in God's mercy
- How great Thou art
- Our God reigns
- The King of love my Shepherd is

Prayers

The intercessions this week could feature prayers for the workplaces of members of the congregation. These could include schools, hospitals, offices and factories – wherever people spend their working lives.

Home-Group Resources

Ice-breaker and Discussion

Encourage the group to discuss whether they've ever experienced the sense of God's speaking to them or encouraging them through someone or something that wasn't explicitly religious. It could have been advice from a friend or family member that was particularly wise; a line in a film or moment in a piece of music that resonated; a piece of art that highlighted something of the goodness of God; or the emotion of shared euphoria at a sports event. Another way of approaching the concept would be to ask people to think about times when they've seen the beauty of creation, and whether that has ever helped shape their understanding of who God is and the good news of Jesus.

The theologian Colin Gunton writes: 'Wherever there is truth, goodness and beauty; wherever things turn out to be what they are created to be, there is to be experienced the work of the perfecting Spirit.'[6] What do people think about this quote? How might the idea behind this shape our everyday witness?

Introducing the theme (to read aloud)

Do you remember the hidden leopards in Johannesburg from Week 4? Can you remember how many hidden leopards were found? It was seven, for those interested! This week, we're delving further into the idea of finding the hidden leopards around us. Throughout **Everyday Witness**, we've focused on witnessing about what God has done and is doing, in and through our lives, and sharing that story with others. Another aspect of being witnesses is sharing what we see God doing in and around us or 'engaging with the place of witness'.

Conversations about religion and faith don't come up in conversation all that regularly. For many people, they are topics that just aren't on their everyday radar. This may lead us to think that we have to crowbar our faith into conversations, which may result in an awkward response from others. It's easy to look for moments to say something about our faith rather than listening intently to the people and places around us. This can make us poor conversation partners and worse witnesses.

Sam Chan, in his book **Evangelism in a Skeptical World**,[6] writes about how the majority of our conversations in life focus on our interests. Particularly in Western culture, we're very happy talking about the news, weather (particularly in England), sport, music, film, TV and so on. The challenge is that many of these interests don't appear to have natural links with ideas of faith. This is because faith and religion draw us from external interests to explore our own values and, ultimately, our world views (the lenses through which we understand all of reality). This distinction between interests, values and world views highlights the crucial role of being witnesses who listen well and ask good questions.

Engaging with the place of witness begins with learning to listen to the people and culture around us, and beginning to understand the values and world views that underpin both what people are interested in and what is popular in culture. We can do so by asking good questions. For example, if someone is a keen runner, we can ask what it is the person values about running and see where the conversation goes. The evangelist Mark Greenwood talks about the importance of seeking to converse with people, not convert people.[7] As we start to know and understand the people around us better, we can begin to witness about what we think God's Spirit is already doing in their lives and where we see the image of God in them. Alternatively, if we are talking about a film or TV show, we can look for the connection points with the gospel in that movie or programme.

Scripture

Read Acts 17.16-34

In this passage, we see Paul offering one example of listening to the culture he finds himself in and seeking a way to connect with that culture. At the start of the reading, Paul is greatly distressed because Athens is full of idols. At first glance, it might look as if there is no connection here with the good news of Jesus. However, in verse 22, Paul says to the people of Athens, 'I see how extremely religious you are in every way.' Despite his distress at the culture, he finds a point of connection.

Activity

You might like to break into smaller groups for this activity. Discuss the idea of discovering connection points with the culture and people around you. Discuss your own interests and which values and world views underpin those interests. Has anyone in the group ever felt similarly distressed about the surrounding culture, as Paul did in Athens? Has anyone ever been able to find the connection points, as we've been describing?

If you have time, ask people to share which current TV shows they enjoy watching. Spend some time reflecting on those programmes. What do they like about them? What are the values being communicated through the shows? Where are the points of connection with the good news of Jesus? Are there any points of conflict with the gospel?

Collect

Lord Jesus, you send us out into your world to be your witnesses in the things we say and do. Grant us the help of the Holy Spirit that we may point people to your love, and so bring glory to you.
Amen.

Prayer

In your prayer time, pray for one another to have eyes to see, ears to hear and the spirit of discernment throughout life.

Looking ahead

Using a journal or notebook, or just an app on your phone, jot down anything that strikes you when experiencing the surrounding culture this week, whether it's while watching films, TV programmes or YouTube videos; listening to the radio; and so on. What are the points of connection with or disconnection from the Christian message? How could you talk to someone about that from your perspective as a witness?

Reflections for Individuals

Readings used in the **Everyday Witness: Reflection Journal** this week:

Monday	Genesis 1.1-5; 26-31
Tuesday	Ruth 1.6-18
Wednesday	Matthew 15.21-28
Thursday	Acts 10.1-33
Friday	Philippians 4.4-9

Week 8
The Power
of Story

Sunday Service Resources

In earlier weeks, we have thought about our own stories and how they relate to the big story of God and our story as the church. This week, we are going to look at the power of story, with a particular emphasis on the story of Paul, as told by Luke in the book of Acts.

Exploring the theme of the service

We have been encouraged to find ways to use stories and testimonies in our services throughout **Everyday Witness**. Rather than having a one-off service in which people share their stories of faith, the aim is to make our churches 'story rich'. There are several ways of doing so.

- Week 5 ('Our Calling to the World') contains details about the 'This Time Tomorrow' slot, which is an excellent way of sharing our stories and contexts in Sunday worship.

- Another approach, which some churches developed for online services during the COVID-19 pandemic lockdown, is to ask different individuals or families to share what God has been doing in their lives on camera (recording for a maximum of five minutes). This encourages, builds up and helps everyone to pray for those people, as well as to understand more of the context in which they and others are called to be witnesses for Jesus Christ.

- When people are reticent or if the occasion demands, writing our stories before we come to a service and offering those stories on a story 'tree' to give thanks for them, pray into them and value each one can be powerful. Many of us think our stories are boring, prosaic or not worth listening to but, when we value each and every one, they can begin to transform our understanding of how our witness about Jesus can help others.

Readings

You may find the lectionary readings are all that you need to focus on these themes. Here are some suggested alternative texts that you could use alongside the lectionary readings:

- Psalm 105 (or some of it)
- 1 Peter 3.8-18a
- Luke 1.46-55

Music

Suitable hymns and songs could include:

- I will sing the wondrous story
- O Christ the same
- And can it be

Prayers

Eucharistic Prayer D from **Common Worship** would be appropriate today.

Home-Group Resources

Introducing the theme *(to read aloud)*

STORIES AND TELLING STORIES ARE FUNDAMENTAL to human relationships. We tell our own and other people's stories, we read biographies, and we watch biopic films or YouTube videos. When you think of the stories of others, what are the things that make them memorable? Spend a few minutes thinking about a story that you found memorable and why, and then share with others in the group. You could make a list of what makes a person's story worth telling, remembering and retelling.

Scripture

Read Acts 9.1-30; 22.3-21; 26.2-23

Alternatively, you might suggest people try to read these beforehand to save time now.

Luke tells Paul's story three times in the book of Acts. Each time it is told slightly differently. What are the key features? Do any of these features connect with or relate to the list you made earlier? What do you find powerful about the stories? What makes them 'work'?

Discussion

The first time we hear the story of Paul's conversion (Acts 9.1-30), it is told to us by Luke, the narrator of Acts. The second and third times, we hear the story from the lips of Paul himself. The story in Acts 9 is one of a series of stories about people coming to faith in Jesus (Simon the greedy magician in Acts 8.9-24; the Ethiopian eunuch in Acts 8.26-39; Saul (Paul) the persecutor, as we've seen; and Cornelius the Roman in Acts 10).

The second telling of Paul's conversion in Acts 22 comes after he has been arrested by the Romans in the temple and the Roman commander allows him to address his fellow Jews.

The third telling, in Acts 26, is Paul speaking, as a Roman citizen, to the Roman authorities in the person of King Agrippa and his court.

Think about these different situations and contexts. What do you notice about the way the three stories are told?

Here are some pointers:

· Paul tells his story with considerable **courage** (notice the result in Acts 22.22-24).

· In Luke 12.11-12, Jesus reassures his followers that even though they will be dragged before rulers and authorities, the **Holy Spirit** will teach them what to say to defend themselves. In Acts 22 and 26, Luke shows us how this is worked out in the life of Paul, as he gives his testimony.

· Paul clearly **tailors** his story to his audience. So he speaks in Aramaic, the language commonly spoken by the Jews at that time (Acts 22.2), calls his audience 'brothers and fathers' (verse 1) and says of himself, 'I am a Jew' (verse 3). But, when speaking with King Agrippa, he explains aspects of Judaism that might not be clear to his audience (for example, he calls the Pharisees the 'strictest sect of our religion' in Acts 26.5).

Activity

In pairs, spend five minutes each telling your story of coming to faith (you may have done this previously but there is real value in growing used to telling it). Now talk with each other about the people you encounter in your daily life. Explain how you might shape your story for those people so that, when you have an opportunity to share it, they can receive it in a way that makes sense to them.

Prayer

Share any updates about the five people you have been praying for, and pray together for them.

Collect

Lord Jesus, you send us out into your world to be your witnesses in the things we say and do. Grant us the help of the Holy Spirit that we may point people to your love, and so bring glory to you.
Amen.

Looking ahead

We will soon be coming to the end of the **Everyday Witness** programme. During the coming week, think about what you have learned and how you plan to keep growing as a witness when the course is over.

Reflections for Individuals

Readings used in the **Everyday Witness: Reflection Journal** this week.

Monday	Acts 8.4-13
Tuesday	2 Samuel 11
Wednesday	Luke 22.14-20
Thursday	Acts 2.14-36
Friday	Luke 10.1-9

Week 9
Sharing in the Joy of God

Sunday Service Resources

The theme for this week is sharing in the joy of God. Our mental image of God may not include the thought that God is joyous. When we think about Jesus, we often picture him as the man of sorrows, taking the suffering of the world into himself. But that's only part of the picture...

Exploring the theme of the service

GOD TAKES JOY IN HIS CREATION, particularly in the creation of humanity, declaring that this is very good. Jesus tells stories in which he likens the kingdom of God to a party – a wedding banquet – and is not averse to contributing to the joy of a literal wedding reception by turning water into wine. The picture of the coming kingdom in the book of Revelation is of a place of joy, where sorrow and sickness are no more, but where healing and peace are our continual experience in the presence of God. The writer of the Hebrews says that Jesus set his face towards the cross because of the joy that was set before him – joy that he takes in having brought us into a new relationship with God. The parables about lost things in Luke 15 make the same point. When something is lost, be it a sheep, a coin or a son, there is grief. But when that thing is found again, there is great joy.

Over the weeks of the **Everyday Witness** journey, we have thought about the ways in which God can use us – all of us – to bring his 'lost' children to him, through telling our stories, sharing our faith and inviting people to church. More importantly, we have begun to put all of this into practice. Perhaps there are already some specific stories to give thanks for: individuals who thought they would never have the confidence to speak about God who have now begun to do so; someone who has accepted an invitation to a church service or event; or prayers that have been answered for one of our five. In this service, it will be important to give thanks for those good things and, perhaps, to give space for one or two of those stories to be told (briefly).

Today, it would also be good to help people to understand the difference between being welcoming to others and inviting others. Almost every church congregation thinks it is welcoming, including those in which visitors feel unwanted. At best, being welcoming is rather passive. Inviting is more active, requiring us to take the initiative. To build on the momentum of **Everyday Witness**, we want people to commit to inviting others, not just being welcoming when visitors come.

Readings

You may find the lectionary readings allow you to focus on these themes. Here are some suggested alternative texts that you could use alongside the lectionary readings:

- Psalm 126
- 1 Peter 1.3–9
- Matthew 22.1–10

Music

Suitable hymns and songs could include:

- And can it be
- How great Thou art
- Joyful, joyful
- Happy day
- Rejoice! The Lord is King
- All for Jesus

Prayers

It would be good to reflect the theme of joyful thanksgiving in the prayers of intercession. **Eucharistic Prayer A** from **Common Worship** might be particularly appropriate.

Home-Group Resources

Read Luke 15:11-31

Introducing the theme *(to read aloud)*

Our mental image of God may not include the thought that God is joyous. When we think about Jesus, we often picture him as the man of sorrows, taking the suffering of the world into himself. But that's only part of the picture. God takes joy in his creation, particularly in the creation of humanity, declaring that this is very good. Jesus tells stories in which he likens the kingdom of God to a party – a wedding banquet – and is not averse to contributing to the joy of a literal wedding reception by turning water into wine. The picture of the coming kingdom in the book of Revelation is of a place of joy, where sorrow and sickness are no more, but where healing and peace are our continual experience in the presence of God. The writer of the Hebrews says that Jesus set his face towards the cross because of the joy that was set before him – joy that he takes in having brought us into a new relationship with God. The parables about lost things in Luke 15 make the same point. When something is lost, be it a sheep, a coin or a son, there is grief. But when that thing is found again, there is great joy.

Discussion

Can you think of a time that you lost something that meant a great deal to you which you later found again? How did you feel? Now look at the reading from Luke 15.11-31. This is one of the best-known of Jesus' parables, the story of the lost son. It builds on the two preceding parables (which, hopefully, you have also read this week): the stories of the lost sheep and the lost coin. (If the group hasn't already read these, perhaps read all of Luke 15 to include these as well.) What do you notice about the attitude and actions of the shepherd, the woman and the father in these stories? What were they feeling when the sheep, the coin and the son were missing? What risks were they prepared to take to find what was lost? How did they react when the lost sheep, coin and son were found again?

To read aloud

That joy is what God feels when one of his children returns to him. Of course, God's children are never completely 'lost' in the sense that God does not know where they are. But they may feel that God is lost to them. They may be unaware of God's love, grace or forgiveness, or the promise of new and eternal life through Jesus. As we have begun to speak about our faith, about church and about God to people around us, so God is reaching out in great love to them. And when they allow themselves to be found by God, there is great rejoicing in heaven.

Activity

This is the last home-group meeting of the **Everyday Witness** journey. So use this time to tell stories and to share how this journey has been for you. What do you have to be joyful about from the past few weeks? And then talk about how you are going to take this forward. What is going to be different in your own life, and perhaps in your church, as a result of **Everyday Witness**? How will you continue to share your faith, to pray for five and to encourage one another? How will you continue to support one another?

Prayer

Now spend some time in thanking God for all that you have shared together. Pray for one another, that God would continue to give you opportunities to speak about him, and courage to take them. Pray for your church to be a place where people come to faith in Christ.

Collect *See page 56.*

Looking ahead

How are you planning to bear witness to Christ in the future? Share your hopes and commitments with one other person and give permission to ask how you are getting on.

Reflections for Individuals

Readings used in the **Everyday Witness: Reflection Journal** this week.

Monday	Luke 15.1-7
Tuesday	Luke 15.8-10
Wednesday	Isaiah 12.1-6
Thursday	Revelation 22.1-6
Friday	Hebrews 12.1-3

Sunday Service Resources

Everyday Witness (the programme) comes to an end today. But our lives as everyday witnesses may be only just beginning.

Exploring the theme of the service

This service has two purposes. First, we want to look back with gratitude. Over the past nine weeks, we have hopefully begun to form some new habits and to observe God at work in the lives of those around us. It will be important to allow space for thankfulness for this in the service. If you have begun to include stories or testimonies in your service, then this would be a day to continue that. If you haven't, perhaps today you could do so, even if only as a one-off.

Equally, it will be important to keep the momentum going. **Everyday Witness** is supposed to be the beginning of something, not the end. Perhaps today would be a good day to launch an Alpha or Pilgrim course, or to distribute invitations to a Christmas or Harvest service for people to give to friends and neighbours. It would also be good to commission everyone as witnesses in their everyday lives; a suggested liturgy for this follows.

Readings

You may find the lectionary readings are all that you need to focus on these themes. Here are some suggested alternative texts that you could use alongside the lectionary readings:

- Isaiah 60.1-5
- Psalm 34.1-8
- Luke 1.46-55

Music

Suitable hymns and songs could include:
- **Look what the Lord has done**
- **I, the Lord of sea and sky (Here I am, Lord)**
- **Go, tell it on the mountain**
- **O for a thousand tongues to sing**
- **Lift high the cross**

Prayers

In the intercessions, it would be good to pray specifically for the witness of your church and all its people, and for people to come to faith in Christ. Eucharistic Prayer D from **Common Worship: Services and Prayers** might be appropriate for this service. The following affirmation of commitment[9] could be used.

Will you continue in the apostles' teaching and fellowship,
in the breaking of bread, and in the prayers?
All   With the help of God, I will.

Will you persevere in resisting evil,
and, whenever you fall into sin, repent and return to the Lord?
All   With the help of God, I will.

Will you proclaim by word and example
the good news of God in Christ?
All   With the help of God, I will.

Will you seek and serve Christ in all people,
loving your neighbour as yourself?
All   With the help of God, I will.

Will you acknowledge Christ's authority over human society,
by prayer for the world and its leaders,
by defending the weak, and by seeking peace and justice?
All   With the help of God, I will.

May Christ dwell in your hearts through faith,
that you may be rooted and grounded in love
and bring forth the fruit of the Spirit.
All   Amen.

Almighty God,
who called your Church to witness
that in Christ you were reconciling the world to yourself:
help us so to proclaim the good news of your love,
that all who hear it may be reconciled to you
through him who died for us and rose again
and reigns with you in the unity of the Holy Spirit,
one God, now and for ever.
All   Amen.

Notes

1   See Elaine Lindridge, **'See what God is doing and join in'**, Theology Everywhere, 21 November 2016, https://theologyeverywhere.org/2016/11/21/see-what-god-is-doing-and-join-in, accessed 13 October 2021.

2   Pope Francis, **Apostolic Exhortation Evangelii Gaudium of the Holy Father Francis to the Bishops, Clergy, Consecrated Persons and the Lay Faithful on the Proclamation of the Gospel in Today's World**, Vatican City: Vatican Press, 2013, pp. 196–7; www.vatican.va/evangelii-gaudium/en/files/assets/basic-html/page196.html, accessed 13 October 2021.

3   Lindridge, **'See what God is doing and join in'** (see Note 1 above).

4   From **Stepping Stones for Growth**, a course from Manchester Diocese, see https://d3hgrlq6yacptf.cloudfront.net/5fbd76bf103bd/content/pages/documents/16104558541424121966.pdf, accessed on 13 October 2021. The story about the hidden leopards is told in one of the videos that accompany the course: 'Video 1: Hidden Leopards'.

5   See Amy Sherman, **'The 6 Ms framework for fruitfulness: a review of Fruitfulness on the Frontlines'** [blog], The Green Room (n.d.), https://greenroomblog.org/2017/01/28/the-6-ms-framework-for-fruitfulness-a-book-review-of-fruitfulness-on-the-frontlines, accessed 13 October 2021.

6   C. Gunton, **The Christian Faith: An Introduction to Christian Doctrine**, Oxford: Blackwell Publishers, 2002, p. 178.

7   S. Chan, **Evangelism in a Skeptical World: How to Make the Unbelievable News about Jesus More Believable**, Grand Rapids, MI: Zondervan, 2018, p.49.

8   Related in a personal conversation.

9   Taken from **'Thanksgiving for the Mission of the Church'**, Common Worship: Daily Prayer, www.churchofengland.org/prayer-and-worship/worship-texts-and-resources/common-worship/daily-prayer/morning-and-evening#mm008e4, accessed 8 October 2021.